The NBA's 10 Greatest Teams Ever

BY HOWARD BLATT

The NBA's 10 Greatest Teams Ever

BY HOWARD BLATT

SCHOLASTIC INC.

New York   Toronto   London   Auckland   Sydney
Mexico City   New Delhi   Hong Kong

PHOTO CREDITS

Cover (Pippen): NBA/Barry Gossage. **Cover (Bird/Johnson), 57, 58, 64, 67:** NBA/Andrew D. Bernstein. **10, 16, 19:** NBA/Dick Raphael. **Cover (Russell), 12, 73, 74, 82, 89, 91:** NBA/Nathaniel S. Butler. **25:** NBA/Ken Regan. **26:** NBA Photo Library. **33, 34, 41:** NBA/Wen Roberts. **42:** NBA/Neil Leifer. **49:** NBA/Jerry Wachter. **50:** NBA/Richard Pilling. **81:** NBA/Jon Soohoo.

PHOTO CREDITS: INSERT SECTION

I (Russell): NBA Photo Library. **II (Chamberlain):** NBA/Ken Regan. **III (Reed), III (West):** NBA/Wen Roberts. **IV (Erving):** NBA/Jerry Wachter. **V (Bird/Johnson), VI (Thomas), VII (Jordan):** NBA/Andrew D. Bernstein. **VIII (Pippen):** NBA/Nathaniel S. Butler.

ISBN 0-590-01090-5

© 1999 by NBA Properties, Inc.
All rights reserved. Published by Scholastic Inc.

12 11 10 9 8 7 6 5 4 3   9/9 0 1 2 3 4/0

Printed in the U.S.A.
First Scholastic printing, February 1999
Book design: Michael Malone

To the greatest of the great, the Bill Russell,
the Wilt Chamberlain, the Michael Jordan,
the Larry Bird, the Magic Johnson
of child wonders, my son, Marc.
—H.B.

TABLE OF CONTENTS

The NBA's 10 Greatest Teams Ever

BY HOWARD BLATT

INTRODUCTION

John Havlicek

A few years ago, when the National Basketball Association celebrated its 50th anniversary, the league conducted balloting among a panel of experts to choose the 50 Greatest Players, Top 10 Coaches and Top 10 Teams in NBA history.

These teams averaged 66 wins per season and posted a cumulative winning percentage of .805. Three teams were selected from the 1960s, one from the 1970s, four from the 1980s and two from the 1990s.

The game has changed much over that period, with more athletically gifted players doing more spectacular things in the air—rising over the rim, throwing down dunks and recording breathtaking blocked shots. But success in the NBA still boils down to character and fundamentals.

To dominate the competition over a regular season and the long postseason road to the NBA Finals, it takes players who accept and embrace their roles within the team scheme. It requires the ability to execute offensively and concentrate defensively, to rise above pressure, to play together unselfishly for the common goal. It takes the willingness to sacrifice personal achievements in the pursuit of a championship ring.

And it takes at least one remarkable superstar player to lead the way.

Consider the Top 10 Teams and the great players who led those special units to glory, often simply by refusing to lose.

Bill Russell (1964–65 Boston Celtics) was the greatest defensive force in the history of basketball and the winner of most of the legendary postseason battles against teams led by the game's greatest offensive force, Wilt Chamberlain. Russell's rebounding triggered the famed Celtic fast break and Boston won an unmatched 11 titles in his 13 seasons.

Wilt Chamberlain (1966–67 Philadelphia 76ers, 1971–72 Los Angeles Lakers) departed from being a one-man offensive show to concentrate on everything else that could be done on a basketball court. And the impact Wilt wielded on these teams' fortunes was greater than when he averaged 50.4 points for a season, in 1961–62 for the Philadelphia Warriors.

Michael Jordan (1991–92 Chicago Bulls, 1995–96 Chicago Bulls) collected his sixth championship ring last spring, after notching his 10th scoring title. He was named regular-season Most Valuable Player for the fifth time and Finals MVP for the sixth time. Jordan's apparent ability to will the Bulls to glory in every full season during which he has competed since 1990–91

Michael Jordan

has established his legacy: the greatest player of all time in any team sport.

Earvin "Magic" Johnson (1986–87 Los Angeles Lakers) revolutionized the point-guard position with his diverse skills, which allowed him to play every position at 6-9, and his gift for motivating teammates to share in his enthusiasm for the game. In '87, he won a regular-season MVP award for the first of three times and the Finals MVP award for the third and last time.

Larry Bird (1985–86 Boston Celtics) was a ball magician with unlimited shooting range and the same capacity for clutch heroics and for making his teammates better as Johnson, his longtime friendly adversary. In 1986, Bird won his third straight regular-season MVP trophy and his second Finals MVP Award.

Moses Malone (1982–83 Philadelphia 76ers) brought a lunch-pail work ethic and an unquenchable drive for offensive rebounds to Philadelphia and changed everything.

Willis Reed (1969–70 New York Knicks) was the heart and soul of the Knicks as their captain. His willful refusal to allow a crippling injury to force him out of Game 7 of the NBA Finals inspired his team to the greatest moment in franchise history.

Isiah Thomas (1988–89 Detroit Pistons) was the gritty, spirited leader and ball distributor on a team that will be remembered as perhaps the toughest, most physical defensive unit in league history.

Great players don't win championships on their own, as Chamberlain and Jordan learned the hard way in their early years as professionals. It takes complementary talent and an ability to balance the desire for personal production against the overriding, overall needs of the team.

But history tells us that a team rarely rises to the top and stakes a claim among history's most cherished without a transcendent, inspirational player showing the way.

In Boston one championship has always been easy to distinguish from the many around it, even though it was the seventh in a string of eight straight Celtics titles that seemed like it would never end.

This time, after the smoke from GM-Coach Red Auerbach's trademark victory cigar had prematurely wafted toward the Boston Garden rafters, the Celtics came within a hair of a shocking, season-ending defeat.

But they were saved by a single, unforgettable moment.

The moment of relief experienced throughout New England was captured by the historic four-word exclamation of raspy-toned Celtics radio-announcing legend Johnny Most. As the final seconds of Game 7 of the Eastern Conference Finals against Wilt Chamberlain and the Philadelphia 76ers ticked away on April 15, 1965, Most shouted:

"Havlicek stole the ball! Havlicek stole the ball!"

And with it, Havlicek stole the series and, for all intents and purposes, the title—because the NBA Finalists from the West, the Los Angeles Lakers, were primed to be defeated without their injured scoring great, Elgin Baylor.

Actually, Havlicek, the Celtics' do-it-all swingman, simply stole back a game that the team seemed to have locked up and then given away just seconds earlier.

With about one minute left in Game 7, Auerbach—a basketball genius with an inclination toward arrogance—had lit up. And why not? The Celtics had a 110–103 lead, thanks to Sam Jones's 37 points and Havlicek's 26.

However, Chamberlain—who had moved from the San Francisco Warriors to Philadelphia that season, but whose postseason nemesis remained the proud and indomitable Russell   scored six straight points, including a slam dunk to make it a 110–109 game with five seconds left.

Then, inbounding the ball from beneath his own basket under duress, a leaping Russell carelessly threw his pass off the basket support (a guy wire running from each side of the backboard to the balcony that existed only at Boston

1964-65 BOSTON CELTICS

	G	FG%	FT%	PPG
Sam Jones	80	.452	.820	25.9
John Havlicek	75	.401	.744	18.3
Bill Russell	78	.438	.573	14.1
Tom Heinsohn	67	.383	.795	13.6
Tom Sanders	80	.429	.745	11.8
Willie Naulls	71	.384	.813	10.5
K. C. Jones	78	.396	.630	8.3
Ron Bonham	37	.414	.821	7.4
Larry Siegfried	72	.415	.779	6.3
Mel Counts	54	.368	.784	4.8
John Thompson	64	.402	.590	3.6
Bob Nordmann	3	.600	n/a	2.0
Gerry Ward	3	.111	1.000	1.7

Tom "Satch" Sanders and Bill Russell helped make the 1964–65 Boston Celtics the stingiest defensive team in the league.

Garden). The ball caromed out of bounds, and Philadelphia had it back with a final shot to win. A devastated Russell fell to one knee, his head in his hands. During the timeout that followed, he pleaded with his teammates to bail him out.

So Havlicek, the remarkable sixth man whose source of boundless energy and basketball instincts made him special, did just that.

Sixers' guard Hal Greer inbounded the ball, in anticipation of getting a return pass and taking the final shot. With the clock ticking off toward a five-second violation, he lobbed the ball toward teammate Chet Walker about 25 feet away, near the top of the key. Havlicek sensed Greer's hesitation, uncoiled, leaped in the air and slapped the ball away. He deflected it to Sam Jones as time ran out on the Sixers.

While Most shouted his four-word sigh of relief again and again, Russell rushed to Havlicek, hugged him and kissed him on the forehead. Then the Boston fans who had charged the court carried away the Celtics legend nicknamed "Hondo" on their shoulders and literally tore off his uniform in wild celebration.

"I couldn't believe it. I lost my voice. I couldn't open my mouth," said Auerbach, so rarely at a loss for words.

Actually, the 1964–65 season began with a tragic loss for the Celtics family and Auerbach, who won the NBA Coach of the Year Award in his next-to-last season on the Celtics bench.

Just a few days before training camp opened, franchise founder Walter Brown died. On Opening Night the team hung a No. 1 in the rafters to honor him and donned the black arm patches they wore all season in his memory. Russell vowed, "We will win the championship for Mr. Brown's memory."

Indeed, the Celtics posted the best record in the East for the ninth straight season. They started off with 11 straight wins. They had a 31–7 mark by New Year's Day. They broke their own NBA record for most victories with a

62–18 mark—14 games better than runner-up Cincinnati.

On the defensive end, Boston leaned on the peerless Russell, along with brilliant guard K.C. Jones and gritty forward Tom "Satch" Sanders. Supported by the scoring of aging forward Tom Heinsohn, Russell also provided 14.1 points and an NBA-best 24.1 rebounds per game.

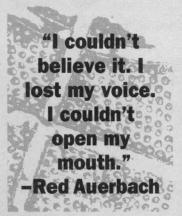

"I couldn't believe it. I lost my voice. I couldn't open my mouth."
–Red Auerbach

Havlicek said of Russell's defensive impact, "On a 3-on-1 break, he could take away the whole floor. He knew the tendencies of everyone involved and, depending on whether the man was right-handed or left-handed, Russell could make him do whatever he didn't want to do. He could take a sequence where there was a 90-percent scoring chance and reduce it to 50 percent. He would say, 'I am going to take away half the floor. Go ahead and see if you can score from the other side.'"

Offensively, the Celtics relied on the radar jump shots and the soft bank shots of Sam Jones, who averaged a team-leading 25.9 points per game during the season and 28.6 points per game during the playoffs. But he was only one of six Celtics who posted a double-figure scoring average that season. Russell, winner of his fifth and final regular-season Most Valuable Player Award, triggered the break, and the tireless Havlicek (18.3 points per game) ran the floor as teams struggled to keep up with the Celtics.

John Havlicek's dramatic, last-second steal sealed the Celtics' Eastern Division Finals victory over the Philadelphia 76ers. In this photo, Lakers legend Jerry West guards Havlicek.

The Celtics and the Sixers split 10 regular-season games and, during the Eastern Division Finals, every team won its home games through the first six.

The Celtics entered Game 7 still lamenting their overtime loss in Game 4, when a buzzer-beating, desperation 35-foot jumper from Greer on an inbounds pass with one second left had forced the extra session that allowed Philadelphia to win, 134–131, at Convention Hall. The stunned Celtics were left wondering out loud, "How could

Greer get his shot off that quickly?"

Russell—who had held Chamberlain to two field goals over the first three quarters in Game 3, not coincidentally a 112–94 Boston victory—had rung up 28 rebounds, 10 blocks, six steals and seven assists in a 114–108 Game 5 victory that gave the Celtics a 3–2 edge in games.

Then, the stubborn Sixers got even again.

But, in Game 7, Havlicek stole the ball. "Havlicek stole the ball!" And the Celtics and their red-faced captain, Russell, dodged a bullet.

"This game went right down to the wire," Russell said slyly, because the happy ending meant that he could joke.

After disposing of the Sixers, the Celtics predictably nailed down their eighth championship of the 11 in the Russell era.

Without Baylor to stoke their offense, the Lakers fell in five games, as anticipated. In the clincher, the Celtics ran off 20 unanswered points as the Lakers were held scoreless for five minutes in a 129–96 rout.

Now Auerbach could light his victory cigar without fear of his team's title going up in smoke.

1965 PLAYOFF RESULTS

(Home team in CAPS)

EASTERN DIVISION FINALS
Boston 4, Philadelphia 3
BOSTON 108, Philadelphia 98
PHILADELPHIA 109, Boston 103
BOSTON 112, Philadelphia 94
PHILADELPHIA 134, Boston 131 (OT)
BOSTON 114, Philadelphia 108
PHILADELPHIA 112, Boston 106
BOSTON 110, Philadelphia 109

NBA FINALS
Boston 4, Los Angeles 1
BOSTON 142, Los Angeles 110
BOSTON 129, Los Angeles 123
LOS ANGELES 126, Boston 105
Boston 112, LOS ANGELES 99
BOSTON 129, Los Angeles 96

1966–67
PHILADELPHIA 76ERS

Wilt Gets His Ring

Wilt "The Big Dipper" Chamberlain was the greatest scoring force that the NBA has ever known. Unstoppable at 7-1, this powerful center set the league record by averaging an outrageous 50.4 points per game over an entire season with the Philadelphia Warriors in 1961–62.

However, for years, while Chamberlain bested Boston great Bill Russell statistically, it was the other way around on the scoreboard when it came to winning the big games. Russell, 4 inches shorter than Wilt, used his quickness to take away Chamberlain's dunks, finger rolls and short bank shots. The Celtics—with eight straight titles—always wound up taking home the rings and the unpopular giant Chamberlain wound up wearing an unfair reputation as a loser in the eyes of fans.

When Alex Hannum came back to Philadelphia as coach for the 1966–67 season, he finally got through to Chamberlain about what the team needed from him to win a championship.

Hannum and Chamberlain had been together before, with the Warriors, and had come to an understanding based on mutual respect after nearly coming to blows during one practice in 1963. Hannum wanted Chamberlain to hit the open man when the defense sagged on him. Wilt, frustrated that he was now 30 years old and still without a championship after the Sixers had lost again to the Celtics in 1965–66, was ready to accommodate.

In 1966–67, Chamberlain averaged only 24.1 points—more than nine points fewer than in 1965–66 on 840 fewer field-goal attempts—and 24.2 rebounds per game. Actually, he was a more efficient scorer than ever, setting the league record with a .683 field goal percentage while allowing the Sixers' offense to flow through him.

The player who had once powered his way to an all-time record 100 points in a single game and who had won league-scoring titles in each of his first seven pro seasons decided to wholeheartedly embrace the team concept. The result was that he made everyone around him better. Wilt averaged 7.8 assists to rank third in the league. Philadelphia mounted an attack that featured six dou-

1966-67 PHILADELPHIA 76ERS

	G	FG%	FT%	PPG
Wilt Chamberlain	81	.683	.441	24.1
Hal Greer	80	.459	.788	22.1
Chet Walker	81	.488	.766	19.3
Billy Cunningham	81	.459	.686	18.5
Wali Jones	81	.431	.838	13.2
Lucious Jackson	81	.438	.759	12.0
Larry Costello	49	.444	.902	7.8
Dave Gambee	63	.435	.856	6.5
Bill Melchionni	73	.391	.650	4.3
Matt Guokas	69	.389	.605	3.0
Bob Weiss	6	.500	.400	2.0

ble-figure scorers en route to 125.2 points per game, still the third-highest mark in NBA history.

"Wilt's presence on the floor made it possible for the other men to be free. Opponents set their defense for Wilt and it left the other men open. Never once did I ask him to shoot less," said Hannum. "He just realizes now that he is playing with a bunch of players who can put the ball in the basket and that he doesn't have to do it himself."

Among the Sixers capable of knocking down the shots that resulted from the defensive traffic around Wilt were dead-eye, jump-shooting guard Hal Greer (22.1 points per game) and slippery Chet "The Jet" Walker (19.3 ppg), who was blessed with an array of moves. And there was sixth man Billy Cunningham, known as the "Kangaroo Kid" because of his jumping ability. Cunningham averaged 18.5 points and 7.3 rebounds in just 26.8 minutes per game as a frontcourt sub.

At power forward, Lucious Jackson did the dirty work, as a staunch defender and Chamberlain's helper on the boards. Hannum brought clever point guard Larry Costello, the last of the NBA's great set shooters, out of retirement to run his offense. When Costello tore an Achilles tendon Jan. 6 and was replaced by Jones, the Sixers were already 38–4.

And, of course, Wilt didn't stop shooting altogether en route to the third of his four regular-season Most Valuable Player awards. In fact, he made 16-of-17 from the floor on Nov. 25 against the Baltimore Bullets. He nailed 15-of-15 against the Los Angeles Lakers Jan. 20 to set an NBA record with a string of 27 straight field goals made. Five weeks later, he broke the record, extending it to 35 in a row over four games, a binge that included a 15-of-15 effort against the Bullets.

The Sixers won 15 of their first 16 en route to a 68–13 finish, the best record in NBA history at the time. They averaged 125.2 points per game and outscored opponents by an average of 10 points per game.

"We had everything—the shooters, the rebounders, the big guy in the middle," said Jackson. "It wasn't so

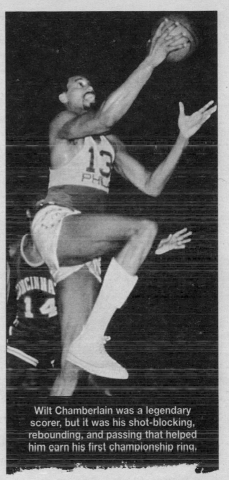

Wilt Chamberlain was a legendary scorer, but it was his shot-blocking, rebounding, and passing that helped him earn his first championship ring.

much a question of winning as how much we were going to win by."

"Those 76ers were so big and strong, but they could beat you with finesse, too," said Jerry West, an All-Star guard for the Los Angeles Lakers.

A ten-time NBA All-Star, guard Hal Greer is the
Philadelphia 76ers all-time leading scorer with 21,586 points.
Here he is guarded by Jerry West.

"It was the greatest aggregation of basketball talent
before or since," said Chamberlain of the unit voted the
number one team in NBA history in 1980, when the league
celebrated its 35th anniversary.

"We had a very compatible team with no petty jeal-
ousies—a team that young men don't know and old men
can't forget," said the Sixers' reserve guard Dave Gambee.

"The whole season was just magical," said Wali Jones.

Of course, the Celtics still stood between the Sixers and

the title that would validate a storybook season. After disposing of Cincinnati in the first round, the Sixers were matched with Russell and Co. again. They were primed to provide a permanent answer to the annoying annual question, "When are you going to beat Boston?"

In Game 1, Chamberlain notched a quadruple-double, with 24 points, 32 rebounds, 13 assists and 12 blocked shots, in a 127–113 victory. Then Greer's clutch jumper in the final seconds of Game 2 lifted the Sixers to a 107–102 win. Philadelphia captured Game 3, too, 115–104, as Chamberlain set a playoff record with 41 rebounds.

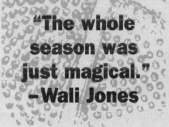

"The whole season was just magical."
–Wali Jones

K.C. Jones, Boston guard, noted the difference in Chamberlain. "They are playing the same game *we've* played for the last nine years—in other words, team ball," he said.

At this point, even Celtics' GM Red Auerbach sensed that Boston was going home early for a change this season.

"Nobody wins all the time except [world heavyweight boxing champion] Muhammad Ali," said Auerbach.

After Boston had salvaged Game 4, the Sixers racked up 75 points in the second half and dethroned the Celtics in a 140–116 Game 5 blowout.

Sixers owner Irv Kosloff recalls the smoke that enveloped Convention Hall in Philadelphia that night. "Everyone lit up a Red Auerbach cigar [his trademark victory celebration smoke] with three minutes left," he said.

After it was over, Russell went to the Philadelphia lock-er room and said just one word to Chamberlain: "Great."

Next came the NBA Finals and a date with the Warriors, led by lethal scorer Rick Barry and defensive-standout center Nate Thurmond.

In Game 1, Chamberlain pulled down 33 rebounds and blocked a shot by Thurmond with four seconds left in reg-ulation as the Sixers emerged with a 141–135 overtime vic-tory after blowing a 19-point lead. Wilt had 38 rebounds in the Sixers' 126–95 Game 2 rout. Then Philly took a 3–1 lead with a 122–108 road win behind Greer's 38 points and Walker's 33. The transformation by Chamberlain and its effects on the team were obvious. Wilt had now scored fewer than 20 points in each of the three Philly wins.

Finally, in Game 6, Chamberlain amassed six blocks and eight rebounds in the fourth quarter alone to lead Philly to a series-clinching 125–122 triumph at the Cow Palace in San Francisco.

After it was over, Hannum, the first coach in NBA histo-ry to win a title with two different teams after having led St. Louis to a championship in 1958, gave Chamberlain the basketball. "You have given of yourself all year so we could get to this moment," said Hannum.

Early the next morning, after a night of wild celebration, Wilt walked slowly through the airport, ball in hand.

1967 PLAYOFF RESULTS
(Home team in CAPS)

EASTERN DIVISION SEMIFINALS
Philadelphia 3, Cincinnati 1
Cincinnati 120, PHILADELPHIA 116
Philadelphia 123, CINCINNATI 102
PHILADELPHIA 121, Cincinnati 106
Philadelphia 112, CINCINNATI 94

EASTERN DIVISION FINALS
Philadelphia 4, Boston 1
PHILADELPHIA 127, Boston 113
Philadelphia 107, BOSTON 102
PHILADELPHIA 115, Boston 104
BOSTON 121, Philadelphia 117
PHILADELPHIA 140, Boston 116

NBA FINALS
Philadelphia 4, San Francisco 2
PHILADELPHIA 141, San Francisco 135(OT)
PHILADELPHIA 126, San Francisco 95
SAN FRANCISCO 130, Philadelphia 124
Philadelphia 122, SAN FRANCISCO 108
San Francisco 117, PHILADELPHIA 109
Philadelphia 125, SAN FRANCISCO 122

1969–70 NEW YORK KNICKS

Captain Courageous

Any story about the 1969–70 Knicks should begin with the dramatic ending, May 8, 1970, Game 7 of the NBA Finals in Madison Square Garden against the Los Angeles Lakers. That was when "The Captain" and heart of the greatest unit in New York basketball history came limping to the emotional rescue of his Knicks.

Willis Reed had been last seen two games earlier—fallen, wincing and twisting in pain, after suffering a severe strain of his right thigh muscle. The Knicks miraculously came from behind to win Game 5 in his absence, but Game 6 was a Lakers rout. Now, the Knicks needed to survive a one-game showdown to take their first title since the NBA was formed in 1946–47.

The Game 7 crowd at Madison Square Garden was buzzing in dismay as the Knicks took their warm-ups. All eyes searched in vain for the missing Reed, the Knicks' leading scorer and only answer to the overwhelming Wilt Chamberlain. Nobody knew for certain if Willis would play.

Suddenly, there was a stirring in the tunnel leading from the Knicks locker room to the floor. The sound grew into a roar, and the Lakers turned to see Reed limping onto the court, his pregame arrival having been delayed by injections of a painkiller and an anti-inflammatory drug. The energy surge was clear. Before Reed removed his warm-ups, the fans in the Garden cheered as though he had just nailed the game-winning shot.

"This is it," Reed had told trainer Danny Whelan. "There is nothing to save up for now."

From the way Reed remained immobile on the opening jump, it looked like he was fit only to be dominated or left crumpled on the floor again. Then, willing himself into the air on his one good leg, Reed somehow hit his first two jump shots for a 5–2 lead as the Garden rafters shook with joy, relief and appreciation. Ignited by their fans, the Knicks surged to a 69–42 halftime lead.

"I have never seen a team so fired up," said Coach Red Holzman.

Those two early baskets represented Willis's only points in the contest. But Reed—the NBA's regular-season, All-

1969–70 NEW YORK KNICKS

	G	FG%	FT%	PPG
Willis Reed	81	.507	.756	21.7
Walt Frazier	77	.518	.748	20.9
Dick Barnett	82	.475	.714	14.9
Dave DeBusschere	79	.451	.688	14.6
Bill Bradley	67	.460	.824	14.5
Cazzie Russell	78	.498	.775	11.5
Dave Stallworth	82	.429	.716	7.8
Mike Riordan	81	.464	.691	7.7
Bill Hosket	36	.505	.788	3.3
Nate Bowman	81	.417	.519	2.9
Don May	37	.386	.947	2.6
Johnny Warren	44	.407	.686	2.5

Star Game and Finals MVP—labored through 27 courageous minutes, harassed Chamberlain into 2-for-9 shooting and frustrated the Lakers' attempt to ride their center.

"I wanted to play," said Willis. "I didn't want to have to look at myself in the mirror 20 years later and say that I had wished I had tried to play."

Walt Frazier, the do-it-all guard, actually carried the Knicks to their 113–99 triumph with a remarkable 36-point, 19-assist effort. But Frazier's game is a footnote to the legend surrounding Willis' entrance that night.

"Just having him out there with us, I got so turned on I couldn't stop," said Frazier. "If that had not happened, I know we would not have won."

Perhaps as no team had been before or has been since, these special Knicks were all about grit, sharing the ball, the defensive stops and the glory. They were truly an odd collection of personalities with differences in style and background. But on the court they blended and, when necessary, even submerged their individual skills to perform with total efficiency.

Reed, the Knicks' proud, soft-spoken, inspirational leader, was a triumph of heart, toughness and will. Drafted in 1964 after every team had passed on him, smoldering with the desire to prove himself, Reed was quick and intelligent, like the great Bill Russell. But Willis possessed a finesse offensive game Russell never had. Reed averaged a team-leading 21.7 points per game on .507 accuracy from the floor in 1969–70.

Dave DeBusschere, acquired from the Detroit Pistons

Center Bill Russell was the primary force behind the greatest streak in NBA history—the Boston Celtics' eight straight championship seasons.

Wilt Chamberlain earned his first championship ring with the 1966-67 Philadelphia 76ers, when he sacrificed personal statistics for the good of the team.

When Willis Reed limped onto
the Madison Square Garden
court for Game 7 of the 1970
NBA Finals, he provided fans
with one of the most emotional
moments in NBA history.

The 1971-72 Los Angeles
Lakers, led by steady guard
Jerry West, embarked on a
remarkable 33-game winning
streak that remains an NBA
record today.

Julius Erving, better known as "Dr. J," changed the game forever with his "above the rim" acrobatics.

Larry Bird and Magic Johnson, of the Celtics and Lakers respectively, brought the NBA to ever-greater popularity—and formed the greatest on-court rivalry since Russell and Chamberlain.

Isiah Thomas provided smooth, slick leadership for the 1988-89 Detroit Pistons—better known by their "Bad Boys" nickname.

In 1991-92, Michael Jordan—soaring to new heights—led a well-rounded Chicago Bulls team to its second championship in two years. There would be more to come.

Scottie Pippen's all-around game provided the perfect complement to "Air" Jordan—and helped the 1995-96 Chicago Bulls attain the greatest single-season record, 72-10, in NBA history.

in the Knicks' all-time best deal, was a no-nonsense, blue-collar grunt and a coach on the floor at power forward.

Bill Bradley was the small forward. The former Princeton legend had a Rhodes Scholarship behind him and glory days as the U.S. senator from New Jersey still ahead of him. An intellectual who dressed and spent money conservatively, he earned the nickname "Dollar Bill." Bradley was not fast and did not possess great leaping ability, but was a deadly catch-and-shoot perimeter shooter and an excellent passer.

Frazier was nicknamed "Clyde" because his wardrobe full of eye-catching furs and fedora hats and his high-profile, man-about-New York City image suggested the dapper gangster who had accompanied Bonnie. The All-Star guard with the lightning hands also showed every bit as

Willis Reed, nicknamed "The Captain," was the heart and soul of the greatest unit in New York basketball history.

much style, swagger and cool with his ball thievery.

Dick Barnett, once a shooter with the Lakers, lived in the shadow of Clyde's flair, just quietly doing everything necessary to help the team win. The gifted, explosive Cazzie Russell offered points off the bench as one of six Knicks to average in double figures that season.

The Knicks surged out of the gate in 1969–70, going 9–1 in October and winning their first 14 in November. In fact, they mounted an NBA-record-breaking 18-game winning streak. Achieving the record in stunning fashion on Nov. 28, the Knicks scored six points in the final 16 seconds, for a 106–105 victory, against the Cincinnati Royals.

Despite the Knicks' league-leading 60–22 regular-sea-

Walt Frazier carried the Knicks to victory in Game 7 of the NBA Finals, with an amazing 36-point, 19-assist performance.

son record, the rings were not guaranteed. They needed to show they had saved their best for the postseason.

Lifted by a 36-point, 36-rebound game by Reed in pivotal Game 5 of the Eastern Division semis, the Knicks outlasted the rugged Baltimore Bullets, with Wes Unseld and Earl Monroe, in a seven-game battle. Then Reed neutralized rookie Lew Alcindor (later known as Kareem Abdul-Jabbar) as the Knicks dismissed the Milwaukee Bucks in five games to reach the Finals.

"I have never seen a team so fired up."
—Red Holzman.

Reed's 37 points—25 in the first half—set the tone in the Knicks' 124–112 Game 1 victory. Then Chamberlain rejected a Reed attempt at a game-tying layup in the final minute of Game 2, saving Los Angeles's 105–103 win.

Game 3 is remembered for Laker All-Star guard Jerry West's answered prayer. With the Knicks ahead, 102–100, on DeBusschere's jumper with three seconds left, West took an inbounds pass from Chamberlain, dribbled three times and nailed a jumper from 60 feet away to send the game into overtime. But the Knicks refused to collapse. Reed (38 points) and DeBusschere (21 points, 15 rebounds) scored all but two of the Knicks' points in the extra period as they won, 111–108.

The Lakers evened the series by winning Game 4, another overtime thriller, 121–115, as West scored 37 points and had 18 assists.

The series' turning point came in Game 5, when the

Knicks rallied behind their injured captain. With the Lakers up, 25–15, late in the first quarter, Reed tripped over Wilt Chamberlain's foot on a drive, went down hard and departed to a hush at the Garden.

So, the Knicks relied on quickness and an improvised offense in rallying from 13 down in the third quarter, using DeBusschere and forward Dave Stallworth in the pivot against Chamberlain. The Knicks forced L.A. into 30 turnovers, 10 in the final quarter. In the second half, they kept West without a field goal and held Wilt to four points to escape with a 107–100 victory and a 3-to-2 series lead.

After the Lakers dominated the Reed-less Knicks in Game 6, the limping Willis and Frazier took care of business in the finale. Clyde made 12 of 17 shots from the floor, all 12 of his free throws, and tied a playoff record held by Celtic legend Bob Cousy with 19 assists.

Fans still embrace the memory of the 1969–70 Knicks. They were special because they played together, played without personal goals, played basketball the way it was meant to be played.

"When we took the floor, we always played as a team," said Bradley. "Players sacrificed individual statistics and glory to make the team the best it could be. Red took a group of players with very different styles and defined us as a team whose sum was truly greater than its parts."

1970 PLAYOFF RESULTS

(Home team in CAPS)

EASTERN DIVISION SEMIFINALS
New York 4, Baltimore 3
NEW YORK 120, Baltimore 117(2 OT)
New York 106, BALTIMORE 99
Baltimore 127, NEW YORK 113
BALTIMORE 102, New York 92
NEW YORK 101, Baltimore 80
BALTIMORE 96, New York 87
NEW YORK 127, Baltimore 114

EASTERN DIVISION FINALS
New York 4, Milwaukee 1
NEW YORK 110, Milwaukee 102
NEW YORK 112, Milwaukee 111
MILWAUKEE 101, New York 96
New York 117, MILWAUKEE 105
NEW YORK 132, Milwaukee 96

NBA FINALS
New York 4, Los Angeles 3
NEW YORK 124, Los Angeles 112
Los Angeles 105, NEW YORK 103
New York 111, LOS ANGELES 108(OT)
LOS ANGELES 121, New York 115(OT)
NEW YORK 107, Los Angeles 100
LOS ANGELES 135, New York 113
NEW YORK 113, Los Angeles 99

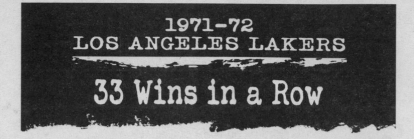

1971-72
LOS ANGELES LAKERS
33 Wins in a Row

The window of championship opportunity seemed ready to close on the Los Angeles Lakers in the fall of 1971.

They had lost to the New York Knicks in the 1970 NBA Finals and they never even made it out of the Western Conference Finals in 1971. Now, the Lakers' three-super-star nucleus looked fragile, even creaky.

All-time great forward Elgin Baylor, in rapid decline, was trying to make it back from knee surgery that had limited him to two games in 1970–71. Amazing center Wilt Chamberlain was 35 years old, and franchise guard Jerry West was 33—both past their prime. Baylor and West had never known the feeling of winning a championship, and Chamberlain had experienced it only once, with the 1966–67 Philadelphia 76ers.

Lakers owner Jack Kent Cooke wanted a ring and was running out of patience. He fired Joe Mullaney as coach and replaced him with former Celtics guard Bill Sharman, who had just captured the 1971 American Basketball Association title as coach of the Utah Stars.

As it turned out, the intense, demanding Sharman was just what the doctor ordered for this team full of frustrated stars and large egos. "We had a lot of players who had personal success but had not enjoyed team success," said West. "We had a lot of very frustrated people."

"Everybody told me, 'You don't want that job,'" recalled Sharman.

And people snickered when Sharman announced he was going to make the Lakers into a running team. But he did.

First, he sold Chamberlain on concentrating on rebounding (19.2 per game in 1971–72), blocking shots and triggering the fast breaks that would get high-scoring guards Gail Goodrich (25.9 points per game) and West (25.8 points and a league-leading 9.7 assists per game) free in the open court.

Wilt, whom Sharman named a Laker co-captain, granted his coach's wish, sacrificing shot attempts and averaging a mere 14.8 points on .649 accuracy. That was a tiny total for

1971-72 LOS ANGELES LAKERS

	G	FG%	FT%	PPG
Gail Goodrich	82	.487	.850	25.9
Jerry West	77	.477	.814	25.8
Jim McMillian	80	.482	.791	18.8
Wilt Chamberlain	82	.649	.422	14.8
Happy Hairston	80	.461	.779	13.1
Elgin Baylor	9	.433	.815	11.8
Flynn Robinson	64	.490	.860	9.9
Pat Riley	67	.447	.743	6.7
John Trapp	58	.443	.699	5.7
Keith Erickson	15	.482	.857	5.7
Leroy Ellis	74	.460	.695	4.6
Jim Cleamons	38	.350	.778	2.6

the player who had averaged an NBA-record 50.4 points per game in 1961–62.

It was not an easy sell for Sharman. "Here I am, the greatest scorer in the history of basketball and I have been asked by my coaches not to score," said Chamberlain. "Now where else in a sport can you ask a guy to stop doing something he's the best in the world at doing? It's like telling Babe Ruth not to hit home runs, just bunt."

Sharman convinced forward Happy Hairston to make the same personal offensive sacrifice, so he could help Wilt more on the boards. And Hairston responded with 13.1 rebounds per game, making him the first forward to average in double figures playing alongside Chamberlain.

The final piece in the Lakers' championship picture fell into place after the season had started. Sharman, convinced that Baylor did not have enough left to play the Lakers' up-tempo style, told Elgin that he was going to start smart, athletic, young small forward Jim McMillian ahead of him. Too proud to come off the bench, Baylor elected to retire after playing just nine games.

The night after Baylor's announcement, Nov. 5, the Lakers beat the Boston Celtics at home and embarked on the remarkable 33-game winning streak that remains an NBA record. With McMillian thriving (18.8 points, 6.5 rebounds per game) and completing the starting five, and reserve guards Pat Riley, Keith Erickson and Flynn Robinson in place, it became clear that Sharman had molded a very special team.

The Lakers seemed positively unbeatable. Of course,

the streak finally ended, on Jan. 9, as L.A. bowed to Milwaukee and Kareem Abdul-Jabbar.

"A lot of the games weren't close," said Sharman, who nevertheless yelled so much that he suffered damage to his voice, which eventually led to his retirement. "It was just an amazing stretch."

The Lakers outscored the opposition by an average of 12.3 points per game that season. They rolled to a 69-13 finish that remained an NBA record until the 1995–96 Bulls bettered it.

But when the playoffs arrived, there were still doubts in some Lakers players' minds.

"We had been so snakebitten in the 1960s, always getting beaten by Boston," said Riley, who would achieve greatness as a coach after his playing career was over. "We were waiting for some-

Anchoring the defense, Wilt Chamberlain became the consummate team-player for the rampaging 1971–72 Los Angeles Lakers.

thing bad to happen again, but it didn't."

Los Angeles eliminated a Chicago Bulls team that had won 57 games in just four, taking advantage of the Bulls' lack of a force at center. Then came the big challenge, in the Western Conference Finals—Abdul-Jabbar and the Bucks. Milwaukee had eliminated Los Angeles a year earlier and had snapped the Lakers' record winning streak during the season.

Adversity reared its head in Game 1 as the Bucks took away the home-court advantage with a 93–72 win at the

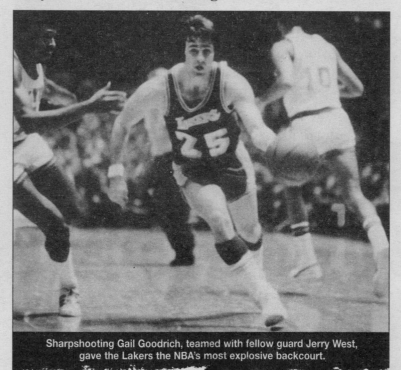

Sharpshooting Gail Goodrich, teamed with fellow guard Jerry West, gave the Lakers the NBA's most explosive backcourt.

Forum, holding the Lakers to 27-percent shooting from the floor overall and only eight points in the third quarter.

Despite West shooting only 10-for-30 from the floor, the Lakers squeezed out a 135–134 win in Game 2. Then they overcame 61-percent shooting by the Bucks to win Game 3 in Milwaukee, 108–105, mostly because Wilt held Abdul-Jabbar (33 points) scoreless for the last 11 minutes. After the Bucks romped in Game 4, the Lakers overcame West's 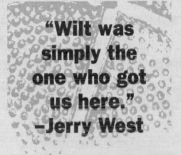 continuing slump to win the next two, 115–90 and 104–100, to close out the series in six games.

Now Los Angeles would have a chance to erase the memory of its bitter seven-game defeat to the Knicks and the hobbled Willis Reed in the 1970 Finals, because a revised collection of Knicks were their opponents in these Finals.

This time, the fates were with the Lakers. Reed was out, and power forward Dave DeBusschere injured his side in Game 2 and was ineffective thereafter. The Knicks won the opener, 114–92, but the Lakers took the next two.

The moment of truth for the Lakers came early in Game 4. Chamberlain fell and sprained his wrist. But he chose to play through the discomfort. Despite pain and foul trouble, Wilt was a shotblocking force in the overtime of a 116–111 victory that gave the Lakers a 3–1 lead in games.

Finally, after originally being expected to be sidelined

for Game 5, Chamberlain took a shot of an anti-inflammatory drug just before the opening tip. The giant, viewed by many in the public as a loser for so long because of so many lost battles with Boston's Bill Russell, wound up scoring 24 points and pulling down 29 rebounds in a 114–100 title-clinching win.

After Wilt had collected the Finals MVP Award, West— who had carried the Lakers for so long but this time was along for the ride during his sub-par postseason—gushed admiration and appreciation. "Wilt was simply the one who got us here," said West.

And Sharman was the man who had reached him.

1972 PLAYOFF RESULTS
(Home team in CAPS)

WESTERN CONFERENCE SEMIFINALS
Los Angeles 4, Chicago 0
LOS ANGELES 95, Chicago 80
LOS ANGELES 131, Chicago 124
Los Angeles 108, CHICAGO 101
Los Angeles 108, CHICAGO 97

WESTERN CONFERENCE FINALS
Los Angeles 4, Milwaukee 2
Milwaukee 93, LOS ANGELES 72
LOS ANGELES 135, Milwaukee 134
Los Angeles 108, MILWAUKEE 105
MILWAUKEE 114, Los Angeles 88
LOS ANGELES 115, Milwaukee 90
Los Angeles 104, MILWAUKEE 100

NBA FINALS
Los Angeles 4, New York 1
New York 114, LOS ANGELES 92
LOS ANGELES 106, New York 92
Los Angeles 107, NEW YORK 96
Los Angeles 116, NEW YORK 111(OT)
LOS ANGELES 114, New York 100

1982-83
PHILADELPHIA 76ERS
Moses and Dr. J

The Philadelphia 76ers had already frustrated their fans and their franchise forward, Julius "Dr. J" Erving, too many times. The Sixers had been to the NBA Finals in 1977, 1980 and 1982 and had lost in six games each time, once to Portland (blowing a 2–0 series lead) and twice to the Lakers.

Erving's magical, soaring flights to the rim and stylish stuffs made him the Michael Jordan of his day. He had won two championships in the since-defunct American Basketball Association, with the New York Nets in 1974 and 1976. But "The Doctor" had no rings to show for his first six seasons of operating in the NBA. He was 32 years old going into the 1982–83 season and wondering if he would ever win one.

"I wanted it badly," he said. "I thought the NBA Championship had eluded me....You don't want to be the answer to a trivia question if you're regarded as one of the all-time best and you do not win a championship."

So Erving was shocked and delighted by the news that broke in the summer of 1982. Philadelphia 76ers owner, Harold Katz, had signed Moses Malone to a six-year contract as a free agent, then dealt center Caldwell Jones and a first-round draft choice to Houston to get the Rockets to waive their rights of matching the deal.

Erving and the rest of the Sixers knew that Malone, the league's premier offensive rebounder and defending regular-season Most Valuable Player, was the centerpiece to their title puzzle. Having dumped the erratic Darryl Dawkins and the hard-working but limited Jones, the Sixers finally had a center to counter the greatness of the Lakers' Kareem Abdul-Jabbar.

"We had everything else," said Erving. "We had the physical talent and the intelligence and the intangibles, like hustle, desire, enthusiasm, love and leadership. We had stars and we had guys who were willing to follow.

"When we got Moses, our focus was very clear about what we had been put together to do, especially after not

1982-83 PHILADELPHIA 76ERS

	G	FG%	FT%	PPG
Moses Malone	78	.501	.761	24.5
Julius Erving	72	.517	.759	21.4
Andrew Toney	81	.501	.788	19.7
Maurice Cheeks	79	.542	.754	12.5
Bobby Jones	74	.543	.793	9.0
Clint Richardson	77	.463	.640	7.6
Clemon Johnson*	32	.500	.586	6.8
Franklin Edwards	81	.472	.761	6.7
Reggie Johnson*	29	.448	.733	5.5
Marc Iavaroni	80	.462	.690	5.1
Russ Schoene	46	.512	.750	5.1
Earl Cureton	73	.419	.493	3.4
Mark McNamara	36	.453	.444	2.2
Mitchell Anderson	13	.364	.333	1.3

* Totals with 76ers only.

having been able to do it in the past. There was an over-riding need, a passion to close the deal. Actually, there was a fear of not doing it, because the window of opportunity was going to close. It was our time."

"What struck me was Moses really wanted to win," said Katz. "I felt he could swallow his ego a little and still score. Not to take anything away from the players we had, but Moses made us special."

> "Not to take anything away from the players we had, but Moses made us special."
> –Harold Katz

"It's Doc's show and I just want to enjoy it," said Malone.

Malone did a whole lot more than watch. The 6-10, 265-pound block of granite, who had jumped successfully from high school to the ABA, led the league in rebounding with 15.3 per game and finished fifth in scoring at 24.5 ppg on .501 shooting in 1982–83. Moses earned regular-season MVP honors for the third time in his NBA career—and Philadelphia went from 20th in the league in rebounding in 1981–82 to first. Malone's 445 offensive boards were 80 more than his closest competitor in the league.

"He was the hard hat," said Erving.

The Sixers were already a talented squad before the arrival of their bull in the middle and sent four players to the 1983 All-Star Game. Four Philadelphia starters—all except rookie forward Marc Iavaroni, the designated pick-setter—plus the super sub Bobby Jones shot better than 50 percent from the floor as the team posted a .499 field goal mark.

Erving made it seven straight seasons of averaging 20 or more points for the Sixers, with 21.4 per game on .517 accuracy. Shooting-guard Andrew Toney, a solid shooter whose career was later cut short by foot injuries, established himself as an All-Star for the first time with a career-high 19.7 points per game. Sixth-man Jones shot 54.3 percent and was

By the 1982-83 season, "Dr. J" had but one burning desire—to win that elusive championship ring.

named to the All-Defensive team for a seventh time, where he was joined by gifted ball distributor and ball thief Maurice Cheeks, who shot 54.2 percent.

The Sixers gave notice to the rest of the league that this time they weren't kidding about finally grabbing those rings. They rushed to a 50–7 record and then wound up 65–17. Coach Billy Cunningham forfeited the Sixers' realistic chance to become the first NBA team to win 70 during the regular season to give his starters a rest and prepare them for the postseason. He knew that this time there could be no excuses.

Still, Malone was suffering from a bad knee and sore tendons going into the postseason, making Cunningham uneasy. The ailments didn't stop Moses from making his famous prediction of Philadelphia playoff domination. In answer to the question of how he expected his team to fare, Moses said, "Fo', fo' and fo." He meant the four wins in each round that were necessary for a title, but folks understood it as a guarantee of three sweeps.

As it turned out, the Sixers

When Moses Malone joined the 76ers in the summer of 1982, his low-post presence turned a very good team... into a champion.

came within a single post-season loss (to Milwaukee in the Eastern Conference Finals), of making that three-sweep scenario come true. By then, Philly had buried the Knicks in four straight, with Malone outscoring the New York center tandem of Bill

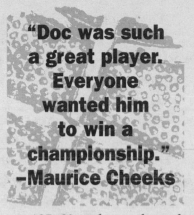

"Doc was such a great player. Everyone wanted him to win a championship." –Maurice Cheeks

Cartwright and Marvin Webster, 125–60 and outrebounding them, 65–36.

The five-game conquest of the Bucks led the Sixers to another NBA Finals, again against the Lakers and their leader, Magic Johnson. This time, Los Angeles was without injured starting forward James Worthy and lost starting guard Norm Nixon plus bench-scorer Bob McAdoo to injury during the course of the Finals.

Still the Lakers were a proud team. And, after having lost the first three games, they made a strong bid to stave off elimination in Game 4 by opening up a 15-point lead in the second half.

That was when, according to Erving, during a timeout Cunningham looked at Moses and said, "If you get every defensive rebound, we can win."

Malone said, "I can do that."

And he did. However, with Los Angeles still holding a 106–104 lead late in the game, it was Erving who addressed another Sixers huddle.

"I'm taking over," he announced.

Then the great Julius stole the ball and dunked, converted a three-point play and nailed a one-hander from the perimeter in Magic Johnson's face to secure a title-clinching 115–108 victory.

"Doc was such a great player. Everyone wanted him to win a championship," said Cheeks.

However, it was Malone who was the unanimous choice as Finals MVP. He outrebounded Abdul-Jabbar, 72–30, and outscored him, 102–94. Malone averaged 26.0 points and 15.8 rebounds overall in 13 playoff games.

"His was silent leadership," said the Sixers' defensive standout forward Bobby Jones. "Moses always had confidence, so you always had confidence because he was always so dominant at his position. Even if things weren't going right for you, you always knew you could depend on Moses, because every night he's going to get rebounds, put it back in or go to the free throw line. That was reassuring."

1983 PLAYOFF RESULTS
(Home team in CAPS)

EASTERN CONFERENCE SEMIFINALS
Philadelphia 4, New York 0
PHILADELPHIA 112, New York 102
PHILADELPHIA 98, New York 91
Philadelphia 107, NEW YORK 105
Philadelphia 105, NEW YORK 102

EASTERN CONFERENCE FINALS
Philadelphia 4, Milwaukee 1
PHILADELPHIA 111, Milwaukee 109(OT)
PHILADELPHIA 87, Milwaukee 81
Philadelphia 104, MILWAUKEE 96
MILWAUKEE 100, Philadelphia 94
PHILADELPHIA 115, Milwaukee 103

NBA FINALS
Philadelphia 4, Los Angeles 0
PHILADELPHIA 113, Los Angeles 107
PHILADELPHIA 103, Los Angeles 93
Philadelphia 111, LOS ANGELES 94
Philadelphia 115, LOS ANGELES 108

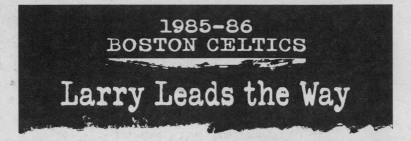

1985-86
BOSTON CELTICS

Larry Leads the Way

The 1985–86 Boston Celtics were the third and last championship team led by Larry Bird, though nobody suspected it at the time—least of all, Bird.

Bird—as important to this era's Celtics as Bill Russell had been to his—overcame his modest capacity for running and jumping with every other imaginable skill. Bird was the game's premier passing forward, with an unmatched vision of the court. He boasted remarkable range on his shot, supreme confidence and court savvy. He was blessed with the ability to make all his teammates better. Plus he had an overwhelming appetite for being the best.

"There has never been and never will be a player like Bird," said longtime coach Chuck Daly.

However, by the beginning of the 1985–86 campaign, Bird was hurting. He had suffered an offseason injury to his back and started the year severely hampered by discomfort. This was the beginning of the back problems that eventually forced his premature retirement in 1992.

"I was in pain all the time," he said. "It affected everything I did. I couldn't bend over or extend myself in any way. I couldn't bend from the waist. If I drove for a shot, I couldn't extend my arm and finish it off. I couldn't take the bumping all the way to the basket."

Still, he did not miss a single game. He worked hard with a physical therapist to condition himself. By midseason, it was clear that Bird would require nobody's sympathy. That sympathy would be more appropriately offered to whomever was given the thankless task of containing him.

On All-Star Weekend, a frisky Bird walked into the locker room and said to his fellow elite, just prior to the NBA's first Three-Point Shooting contest: "OK, which one of you guys plans on finishing second?"

Then he obliterated the field.

On Feb. 14, Bird scored 47 points—including the game-winning basket—and had 14 rebounds and 11 assists in a 120-119 Celtics win in overtime at Portland. Bird made 10 of his 21 baskets with his left hand and joked afterwards, "I

1985-86 BOSTON CELTICS

	G	FG%	FT%	PPG
Larry Bird	82	.496	.896	25.8
Kevin McHale	68	.574	.776	21.3
Robert Parish	81	.549	.731	16.1
Dennis Johnson	78	.455	.818	15.6
Danny Ainge	80	.504	.904	10.7
Scott Wedman	79	.473	.662	8.0
Bill Walton	80	.562	.713	7.6
Jerry Sichting	82	.570	.924	6.5
David Thirdkill	49	.491	.625	3.3
Sam Vincent	57	.364	.929	3.2
Sly Williams	6	.238	.583	2.8
Rick Carlisle	77	.487	.652	2.6
Greg Kite	64	.374	.385	1.3

am saving the right hand for the Lakers."

For the season, Bird averaged 25.8 points, 9.8 rebounds, 6.8 assists and 2.02 steals. He converted 42.3–percent of his three-point attempts and a league-leading 89.6–percent of his free-throw chances. Bird won the NBA's regular-season Most Valuable Player Award for the third straight season.

Not only was Bird soaring at the height of his powers in 1985–86, his supporting cast was never more splendid.

There was Robert Parish in the middle, playing tireless defense and nailing that awkward-looking, high-arcing jumper from short range to the tune of 16.1 points per game and a .549 field-goal percentage.

There was unstoppable low-post force Kevin McHale, a two-time NBA Sixth Man of the Year. The bony forward with the coat-hanger shoulders was a starter for the first time and responded with 21.3 points per game and .574 shooting, the fifth-best mark in the league. Despite missing 14 games with a sore Achilles tendon, McHale used his long arms to block 134 shots during the season and 43 in the playoffs.

At the point-guard spot was the defensively brilliant Dennis Johnson (15.6 points per game), who had won a title in Seattle. Johnson's backcourt mate was the gritty Danny Ainge, who scored 10.7 per game on .504 shooting, including .356 on threes.

The Boston bench was well-stocked, too. Low-key coach K. C. Jones had lost faith in his reserves in 1984–85, when the Celtics suffered a humbling six-game defeat to Los

Angeles in the Finals. So management went shopping.

Bill Walton, with a history of severe foot problems and a championship with Portland under his belt, was imported from the Los Angeles Clippers for Cedric Maxwell and a first-round draft choice. Walton had missed three full seasons and chunks of others with injuries. But, in 1985–86, Bill played in all but two of Boston's 82 regular-season games and all 18 playoff games.

The rejuvenated Walton showed the skills that earned him recognition as the premier passing center in the game with 165 assists and shot .562 from the floor as Parish's backup. Leader of the second unit—which included sharpshooter Jerry Sichting and former All-Star forward Scott Wedman— Walton was a perfect fit with the Celtics, who built their legend on fast breaks and unselfish team play. The big

Bill Walton, guarded by Kareem Abdul-Jabbar, capped an injury-plagued career when he became a "super-sub" for the Boston Celtics—helping them win yet another NBA title.

Larry Legend, averaging 25.8 ppg in 1985–86, did everything well, but one thing beyond all else—he made those around him better.

redhead was named NBA Sixth Man of the Year.

"Bill Walton made everyone on the second team twice as good as they really were," said Bird.

The Celtics lost their season opener, then won 17 of 18. They had winning streaks of 13 and 14 games en route to the fourth-best winning percentage ever at .817, and their

67–15 mark was the second-best record in franchise history. They set a league record for home-court excellence with a 40–1 record (.976) at the Boston Garden.

The Celtics swept the Chicago Bulls in the opening round of the playoffs, despite awe-inspiring performances of 49 and 63 points by Michael Jordan. Boston then ousted the Atlanta Hawks in five games, outscoring the Hawks, 36–6, in the third quarter of Game 5. The Celtics went on to punish the Milwaukee Bucks in a four-game sweep in the Eastern Conference Finals.

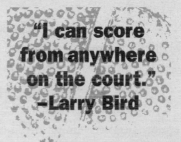

"I can score from anywhere on the court."
–Larry Bird

One last obstacle remained—the Houston Rockets, featuring Twin Towers Hakeem Olajuwon and Ralph Sampson.

Bird had 21 points, 13 assists, eight rebounds and four steals, and the Celtics shot 66 percent in a 112–100 Game 1 win. Bird then notched 31 points, eight rebounds, seven assists and four steals in a 117–95 Game 2 romp. After Houston notched a 106–104 Game 3 triumph, Boston took a 3–1 series lead behind Parish's 22 points and 10 rebounds in a 106–103 victory.

A fight broke out between Sichting and Ralph Sampson in Game 5 and both players were ejected. The fired-up Rockets prevailed to force Game 6 in Boston.

In that game, Sampson seemed intimidated by the angry Boston crowd, missing his first seven shots. But it is highly doubtful that the Rockets could have won even if Sampson had been brilliant instead of awful.

Bird simply would not have permitted it.

Larry Legend rang up 29 points, 11 rebounds and 12 assists and even won a jump ball against Olajuwon as Boston won its 16th title, 114–97. Bird won his second Finals MVP Award.

"I just saw him [Bird] take on five men by himself," marveled Houston reserve Jim Petersen.

It was just a brilliant show from a one-of-a-kind player at his peak. "I just felt there was no one in the league who would guard me if I was playing hard," said Bird. "Once I'm near the three-point line, I can score from anywhere on the court. It's hard to stop a guy who has unlimited range."

1986 PLAYOFF RESULTS
(Home team in CAPS)

EASTERN CONFERENCE
FIRST ROUND
Boston 3, Chicago 0
BOSTON 123, Chicago 104
BOSTON 135, Chicago 131(2OT)
Boston 122, CHICAGO 104

EASTERN CONFERENCE
SEMIFINALS
Boston 4, Atlanta 1
BOSTON 103, Atlanta 91
BOSTON 119, Atlanta 108
Boston 111, ATLANTA 107
ATLANTA 106, Boston 94
BOSTON 132, Atlanta 99

EASTERN CONFERENCE FINALS
Boston 4, Milwaukee 0
BOSTON 128, Milwaukee 96
BOSTON 122, Milwaukee 111
Boston 111, MILWAUKEE 107
Boston 111, MILWAUKEE 98

NBA FINALS
Boston 4, Houston 2
BOSTON 112, Houston 100
BOSTON 117, Houston 95
HOUSTON 106, Boston 104
Boston 106, HOUSTON 103
HOUSTON 111, Boston 96
BOSTON 114, Houston 97

61

1986-87
LOS ANGELES LAKERS

Pure Magic

The shot is remembered with joy in Los Angeles and sadness in Boston. It was the time when Magic Johnson gave the Celtics the hook—a junior sky-hook that was the moment of truth in another classic playoff struggle.

The Lakers, their relentless coach Pat Riley and their peerless point guard Johnson especially, had been on a mission all season. They were determined to carve out another ending like the title-winning ones they had in 1979–80, 1981–82 and 1984–85. They were galled by the way the previous season had ended—with the Celtics cruising to a title behind double-MVP Larry Bird, after the Lakers had suffered elimination at the hands of the Houston Rockets in the Western Conference Finals.

The 1986–87 Lakers rode the brilliance of Johnson and their unique, flamboyant, exciting fast-break style— dubbed "Showtime"—to a 65–17 regular-season record. Then they drove to the Finals with 11 victories in 12 playoff games. Now Bird's Celtics awaited them, a matchup that delighted the world's basketball fans. In every year since Bird and Magic had entered the league in 1979, either the Celtics or the Lakers reached the Finals. The teams had split their two Finals encounters, in 1984 and 1985.

And now Boston was presenting a real challenge to Los Angeles' championship plans.

The Celtics were ahead, 106–105, in Game 4 of the 1987 Finals at the Boston Garden—on the strength of a go-ahead, three-point shot by Bird with 12 seconds left. Boston was now five seconds away from evening the series at two games apiece with a victory, but the Lakers had one final shot.

The first option was to get it to center Kareem Abdul-Jabbar for the shot, but Magic was supposed to make something happen for himself if Abdul-Jabbar was covered. After Magic took the inbounds pass, big Kevin McHale switched over to defend him. Magic faked toward the baseline and came across the middle as Bird and center Robert Parish closed in.

Magic went with what he considered the most unblock-

1986-87 LOS ANGELES LAKERS

	G	FG%	FT%	PPG
Magic Johnson	80	.522	.848	23.9
James Worthy	82	.539	.751	19.4
Kareem Abdul-Jabbar	78	.564	.714	17.5
Byron Scott	82	.489	.892	17.0
A. C. Green	79	.538	.780	10.8
Michael Cooper	82	.438	.851	10.5
Mychal Thompson*	33	.480	.743	10.1
Kurt Rambis	78	.521	.764	5.7
Billy Thompson	59	.544	.649	5.6
Adrian Branch	32	.500	.778	4.3
Wes Matthews	50	.476	.806	4.2
Frank Brickowski	37	.564	.678	3.9
Mike Smrek	35	.500	.640	2.2

* Totals with Lakers only.

able shot in his arsenal—"the junior, junior sky-hook"—a version of the high-arcing shot that he had learned from Abdul-Jabbar. It just cleared Parish's outstretched fingertips; *swish* with two seconds left.

"You expect to lose on a sky-hook," said Bird, who missed the Celtics' final shot in a 107–106 defeat that gave the Lakers a commanding 3–1 edge in games and propelled them toward their eventual six-game triumph. "You don't expect it to be from Magic."

"Everybody thought I couldn't score," said Magic. "I had said, 'I am just going to go along and one of these days, it is going to be my show.' That shot proved it to everybody

On a Lakers roster studded with stars, regular-season and Finals MVP Magic Johnson shined the brightest of them all.

and that was the year I won MVP. That's the year Pat said, 'OK, Earvin, I want you to take over.' And that's what happened. After that, people said, 'It is Larry *and* Magic'; instead of 'Larry can do this and Magic can't do that.'"

Indeed, at the start of 1986–87, Riley took the chief offensive load off the shoulders of the aging Abdul-Jabbar

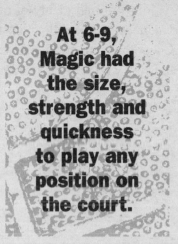

At 6-9, Magic had the size, strength and quickness to play any position on the court.

and put it squarely on Magic's. Magic had been working on his outside shooting since he entered the league and was now a reliable threat from 20 feet. Johnson was being turned loose to shoot more often. The Lakers were his team to carry offensively.

During a three-game span in the regular season when Abdul-Jabbar was out with an eye infection, Magic averaged 39.3 ppg and 13.3 assists. On Dec. 23, 1986, Magic scored a career-high 46 points against Seattle in an overtime win. Magic averaged a career-high 23.9 ppg on .522 shooting from the floor and a league-high 12.2 assists.

The 6-9 Johnson had the size, strength and quickness to play any position on the court and was unmatched in his ability to find his teammates with passes. Magic won his first regular-season MVP Award, becoming the first guard since Oscar Robertson to win it and breaking Bird's three-year hold on the honor.

Johnson had plenty of quality running mates, as all five Laker starters, sixth man and defensive-specialist Michael Cooper and important midseason addition Mychal Thompson finished with scoring averages in double figures.

"Magic is the best player I've ever seen." –Larry Bird

All-Star forward James Worthy (19.4 points per game on .539 accuracy), shooting guard Byron Scott and Cooper were deadly on the break. Abdul-Jabbar (17.5 points per game on .564 shooting), already the NBA's all-time career point producer, was still a formidable scoring threat in the low post.

A. C. Green did lots of dirty work up front. Cooper, the NBA's Defensive Player of the Year, did as good a job as anyone hounding Bird. And, as a backup center and power forward, Thompson gave Riley another big body to use in matching up with the Celtics' giant front line.

The Lakers' regular season and the eliminations of Denver, Golden State and Seattle in one more than the minimum number of games were just a prelude to the Finals and the latest Magic-Bird head-to-head.

In Game 1, Johnson had 29 points, 13 assists, eight rebounds and no turnovers and Worthy scored 33. The Lakers amassed 35 fast breaks in the first half alone and led by 21 at the break en route to a 126–113 win.

In the next game, with the Celtics concentrating on Magic, Cooper went on a tear. He either scored or assisted on every Laker point during a 20–10 run in the second quarter, notching eight assists in the period to tie a Finals record. Cooper made six three-pointers overall, and Magic racked up 22 points and 20 assists in a 141–122 Laker rout.

When Boston won Game 3 and led Game 4 by 16 at half-

A 19-time NBA All-Star and proud owner of six championship rings, Kareem Abdul-Jabbar finished his career with 38,387 points— an NBA record.

time, the home crowd sensed the tide was turning in the Celtics' favor. Then came the Lakers' second-half comeback and that fateful, devastating Magic sky-hook that silenced the Garden fans.

Despite Magic's 29 points, 12 assists, eight rebounds and four steals in Game 5, the Celtics prevailed and stayed alive. However, in Game 6, Abdul-Jabbar had 32 points, six rebounds and four blocks and Johnson notched 16 points, 19 assists and eight rebounds as L.A. won its fourth title in the Magic era.

"This team is fast, can shoot and rebound," said Johnson. "We've got inside people. I have never played on a team that had everything before."

By being named playoff MVP for the third time, Magic had duplicated Bird's double-MVP (regular season and playoff) coup of the season before. To date, Magic, Bird, Willis Reed, Moses Malone, Michael Jordan and Hakeem Olajuwon are the only players in history to accomplish that feat.

"Larry and I motivate each other," said Magic. "He had won MVP three times—and I wanted to show I could win it. He is my measuring stick. Nobody draws everything out of me like Boston and Larry."

"Magic is the best player I've ever seen," said the gracious Bird.

"We wouldn't be anywhere without him," said the grateful Riley.

1987 PLAYOFF RESULTS

(Home team in CAPS)

**WESTERN CONFERENCE
FIRST ROUND**
Los Angeles 3, Denver 0
LOS ANGELES 128, Denver 95
LOS ANGELES 139, Denver 127
Los Angeles 140, DENVER 103

**WESTERN CONFERENCE
SEMIFINALS**
Los Angeles 4, Golden State 1
LOS ANGELES 125, Golden State 116
LOS ANGELES 116, Golden State 101
Los Angeles 133, GOLDEN STATE 108
GOLDEN STATE 129, Los Angeles 121
LOS ANGELES 118, Golden State 106

**WESTERN CONFERENCE
SEMIFINALS**
Los Angeles 4, Seattle 0
LOS ANGELES 92, Seattle 87
LOS ANGELES 112, Seattle 104
Los Angeles 122, SEATTLE 121
Los Angeles 133, SEATTLE 102

NBA FINALS
Los Angeles 4, Boston 2
LOS ANGELES 126, Boston 113
LOS ANGELES 141, Boston 122
BOSTON 109, Los Angeles 103
Los Angeles 107, BOSTON 106
BOSTON 123, Los Angeles 108
LOS ANGELES 106, Boston 93

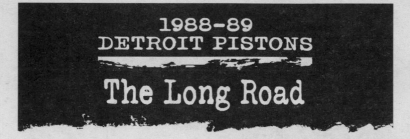

1988-89 DETROIT PISTONS
The Long Road

For many years, in fact the entire time they had been in the league, from 1948 through the 1987–88 season, the Pistons did not win a championship. At that time, no other team had been in the NBA that long without winning a title.

In the mid-1980s they consistently failed to get past the Boston Celtics to graduate to the Finals. And, after the Pistons had finally subdued Boston in 1987–88, the Lakers came from behind to beat them in the Finals.

The patience of this hard-luck team with championship aspirations was nearly exhausted by playoff failure after playoff failure. The Pistons were dedicated to making 1988–89—the team's first year in its new state-of-the-art arena, The Palace of Auburn Hills—memorable as the season they finally broke through to greatness.

Chuck Daly's team was gritty and gifted, built around solid frontcourt players and sharp-shooting guards.

The emphasis on defense began with role-playing center Bill Laimbeer (13.7 points on .499 accuracy, 9.6 rebounds), who set the tone with his all-out hustle and whose burning desire to win rubbed off on his teammates. Alongside Laimbeer were power forward Rick Mahorn, jumping jack John Salley and Dennis Rodman. Rodman, already carving out his niche as a defensive and rebounding force, hardly ever looked for his shot, but made a team-leading 59.5 percent of his attempts in 1988–89.

"When Rodman is on his game, he is worth a difference of 10 points per game," said Daly, whose team defense permitted only 100.8 points per game in 1998–89.

The Pistons were a team on a mission that season, having come so close to winning the title in 1988. The defending Eastern Conference champions frustrated opponents all season long with their defensive intensity and their will to win.

Of course, these Pistons had a whole lot going for them

1988-89 DETROIT PISTONS

	G	FG%	FT%	PPG
Adrian Dantley*	42	.521	.839	18.4
Isiah Thomas	80	.464	.818	18.2
Joe Dumars	69	.505	.850	17.2
Mark Aguirre*	36	.483	.738	15.5
Vinnie Johnson	82	.464	.734	13.8
Bill Laimbeer	81	.499	.840	13.7
Dennis Rodman	82	.595	.626	9.0
James Edwards	76	.500	.686	7.3
Rick Mahorn	72	.517	.748	7.3
John Salley	67	.498	.692	7.0
Micheal Williams	49	.364	.660	2.6
John Long*	24	.475	.846	2.0
Darryl Dawkins	14	.474	.500	1.9
Steve Harris	3	.250	1.000	1.3
Fennis Dembo	31	.333	.800	1.2
Pace Mannion*	5	1.000	n/a	0.8
Jim Rowinski*	6	.000	1.000	0.7

* Totals with Pistons only.

beyond defensive muscle. There was plenty of offensive finesse, beginning with the two starting guards: the bolt-quick penetrator Thomas (18.2 points, 8.3 assists per game) and the versatile Joe Dumars (17.2 points on .505 shooting). Vinnie Johnson (13.8 points) was nicknamed "The Microwave" because he heated up so quickly coming in cold off the bench. And backup center James Edwards was the low-post scoring threat that Laimbeer was not.

"We wanted it more than anyone else." –Bill Laimbeer

But the move that played the biggest part in transforming these Pistons from wannabes into champions was the Feb. 15 trade of high-scoring, post-up small forward Adrian Dantley to Dallas with a number-one draft pick for Mark Aguirre. Because Aguirre was a player with a reputation for being selfish and hard to motivate, the deal was initially unpopular in Detroit.

However, Dantley was uncomfortable with Daly's insistence on playing a more up-tempo game in 1988–89, and Aguirre was delighted to be part of a winning unit. He averaged 15.5 points for the Pistons and did everything he could to fit in. The trade triggered a 30–4 closing run by Detroit that included a 16–1 record in March and a string of 21 straight home wins. The Pistons surged past Cleveland to a Central Division crown and a franchise-best record of 63–19.

Then the Pistons swept the Boston Celtics and Larry Bird, who had missed most of the season with a heel injury, and took the Milwaukee Bucks in four straight games. They required six games to wear down Michael Jordan with their relentless defense and dispose of the Chicago Bulls, but the Pistons were back in the Finals.

The Lakers were back in the Finals, too, as winners of 11 straight postseason games and in hot pursuit of their third straight title, in 42-year-old Kareem Abdul-Jabbar's final season.

"We have an unusually large number of mentally strong players on this team," said Laimbeer. "Make no mistake— we did learn from Boston the past few years about how far

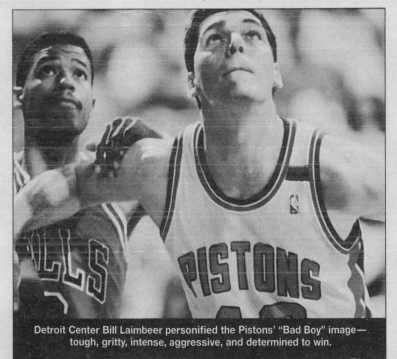

Detroit Center Bill Laimbeer personified the Pistons' "Bad Boy" image— tough, gritty, intense, aggressive, and determined to win.

mental toughness can carry you. They were the champions of that every year.... L.A. has our rings and we want our own rings. That is enough incentive right there."

It promised to be a delicious rematch. But, as the fates had it, the Pistons simply rolled over a wounded Los Angeles team. First, Los Angeles shooting guard Byron Scott suffered a severe hamstring injury in practice before Game 1 and wound up missing the whole series. Then, in Game 2, Magic Johnson suffered a severe hamstring pull of his own with 4:39 left in the third quarter, which— except for a five-minute failed attempt to compete in Game 3—ended his season.

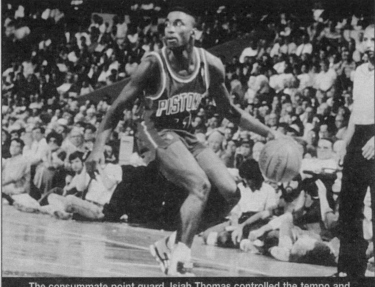

The consummate point guard, Isiah Thomas controlled the tempo and simply did whatever it took—taking the big shot, making the clutch steal, hitting the open man—to lead his team to victory.

"I don't know what it [the injuries] means to them and I don't care," said Thomas. "They didn't care about me last year when I was hurt."

Isiah scored 24 points, Dumars 22 and Johnson 19 in a 109–97 Game 1 victory for Detroit as Mahorn harassed All-Star forward James Worthy into 6-for-18 shooting. The Pistons rallied from a 90–81 hole in Game 2 to pull out a 108–105 victory, behind Dumars' 33-point effort and thanks to a missed free throw by Worthy that could have tied it and forced an overtime.

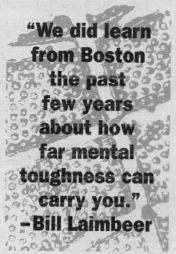

"We did learn from Boston the past few years about how far mental toughness can carry you."
–Bill Laimbeer

In Game 3, Thomas had 26 points and eight assists, the sore-backed Rodman pulled down 19 rebounds and Dumars scored 31 points, including a stretch of 17 straight during his 21-point third quarter. Then, with the Lakers down 113–110 and in need of a three-pointer from rookie point guard David Rivers to tie in the final seconds, Dumars came out of nowhere to block the shot and save the ball from going out of bounds in a 114–110 win.

"I can't even think of the last time I blocked a shot. It was just instinct," said Dumars.

The play sealed the Finals MVP Award for Dumars, who had been a disappointment in the 1988 Finals and had missed 12 games during 1988–89 with a broken hand. In these Finals, Dumars—who often played in the shadow of his All-Star backcourt partner Isiah Thomas—averaged 27.3 points per game on just short of 58-percent shooting.

In Game 4, Detroit trailed by as much as 16 before reality reasserted itself. It was Abdul-Jabbar's final game, but the Pistons remember it as the night they finally got the monkey off their backs. As the final seconds ticked off on a 105–97 sweep-securing victory, Mahorn waved a towel and Thomas sent the ball zipping toward the rafters.

"It means so much, so much," said Thomas, who cried and kissed and hugged the championship trophy. "Winning four [in the Finals] is much sweeter after you have lost four. Believe me."

"We wanted it more than anyone else," said Laimbeer.

1989 PLAYOFF RESULTS
(Home team in CAPS)

EASTERN CONFERENCE FIRST ROUND
Detroit 3, Boston 0
DETROIT 101, Boston 91
DETROIT 102, Boston 95
Detroit 100, BOSTON 85

EASTERN CONFERENCE SEMIFINALS
Detroit 4, Milwaukee 0
DETROIT 85, Milwaukee 80
DETROIT 112, Milwaukee 92
Detroit 110, MILWAUKEE 90
Detroit 96, MILWAUKEE 94

EASTERN CONFERENCE FINALS
Detroit 4, Chicago 2
Chicago 94, DETROIT 88
DETROIT 100, Chicago 91
CHICAGO 99, Detroit 97
Detroit 86, CHICAGO 80
DETROIT 94, Chicago 85
Detroit 103, CHICAGO 94

NBA FINALS
Detroit 4, Los Angeles 0
DETROIT 109, Los Angeles 97
DETROIT 108, Los Angeles 105
Detroit 114, LOS ANGELES 110
Detroit 105, LOS ANGELES 97

Michael Refuses to Lose

The 1991–92 Chicago Bulls knew they were championship material. They had rings to prove it. They had earned them, at last, the previous spring by exploding past the Detroit Pistons, a perennial stumbling block, and Magic Johnson's Los Angeles Lakers for the first title of Michael Jordan's career.

Now Jordan was recognized not only for his greatness but also for his ability to lead a team to a championship, like Magic and Larry Bird. So Air Jordan's new challenge was mustering the resolve for a repeat. For the Bulls to join the Boston Celtics, the Lakers and the Pistons as the only NBA franchises to win titles back to back, his Airness and Scottie Pippen had to find the inspiration and the focus to lead the Bulls to the top again.

Arguably the greatest two-player tandem in NBA history, the versatile Jordan and Pippen were at their height in 1991–92. Together, they averaged 51 points, 14 rebounds, 13 assists and four steals and used their quickness and their leaping ability to create havoc in the opposition's passing lanes.

Complementary role players such as rebounder Horace Grant (14.2 points per game on .578 shooting plus 10.0

rebounds), stop-and-pop jump shooters such as John Paxson and B. J. Armstrong, plus the rugged three-headed center of Bill Cartwright, Will Perdue and Scott Williams supported the dynamic duo.

However, it always came back to Jordan and Pippen as the keys to Coach Phil Jackson's triangle offense and pressing defense.

"There have never been a pair of bookend players like Pippen and Jordan, never two guys as multidimensional," says Orlando Magic Executive Vice President Pat Williams. "They can be whatever they want to be."

"I've always thought Michael and anybody are the greatest tandem," said Knicks GM Ernie Grunfeld. "Pippen, though, is not just anybody."

1991-92 CHICAGO BULLS

	G	FG%	FT%	PPG
Michael Jordan	80	.619	.832	30.1
Scottie Pippen	82	.506	.760	21.0
Horace Grant	81	.578	.741	14.2
B. J. Armstrong	82	.481	.806	9.9
Bill Cartwright	64	.467	.604	8.0
John Paxson	79	.528	.784	7.0
Stacey King	79	.506	.753	7.0
Will Perdue	77	.547	.495	4.5
Craig Hodges	56	.384	.941	4.3
Cliff Levingston	79	.498	.625	3.9
Scott Williams	63	.483	.649	3.4
Bobby Hansen*	66	.444	.364	2.5
Mark Randall	15	.455	.750	1.7
Dennis Hopson	2	.500	n/a	1.0
Rory Sparrow	4	.125	n/a	0.8
Chuck Nevitt	4	.333	n/a	0.5

* Totals with Bulls only.

"No one has scored better or easier than Michael Jordan and I don't know if anyone the size of Scottie Pippen has had a better floor game outside of Larry Bird or Magic Johnson," said Jackson.

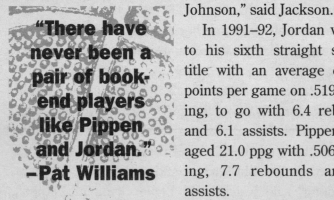

**"There have never been a pair of book-end players like Pippen and Jordan."
–Pat Williams**

In 1991–92, Jordan waltzed to his sixth straight scoring title with an average of 30.1 points per game on .519 shooting, to go with 6.4 rebounds and 6.1 assists. Pippen averaged 21.0 ppg with .506 shooting, 7.7 rebounds and 7.0 assists.

The Bulls won a club-record 67 games, 10 more than any other NBA team won that year. And the 1991–92 Bulls' average victory margin of 10.4 points was the largest in the NBA in 20 years.

Chicago set a club record by winning 31 road games and matched the franchise's best home record at 36–5. The Bulls reeled off a club-record string of 14 triumphs in a row from Nov. 6 through Dec. 6 to begin the season at 15–2. Later, the Bulls won 13 straight, between Jan. 4 and Jan. 25, pushing their record to 37–5. As chillingly effective running their offense as they were deadly on the defensive end, the Bulls finished first in the league in field goal percentage at .508 and averaged 109.9 points per game.

The Bulls did not peak for the postseason. They overcame. First, they swept the Miami Heat, 3–0, in the first round as Michael Jordan led the way with 56 points in the clincher. But then the series against the New York Knicks, the Cleveland Cavaliers and the Portland Trail Blazers were all dogfights.

"We cruised through the regular season and, after the first round, it was a struggle," said Paxson.

"We lost concentration the last two weeks of the regular season and kind of sauntered into the playoffs," said Jackson. "Ultimately, we got to the Knicks series and we

Widely recognized as the greatest to ever play the game, by the 1991–92 season Michael Jordan was also known for one more thing—his ability to lead a team to a championship.

got our chops burned in Game 1 [a 94–89 loss]."

Jordan set a new team playoff record by running off 15 consecutive points in the first quarter of an 86–78 Game 2 victory over the Knicks. The Bulls regained their home-court edge by taking Game 3 on the road, 94–86. Then the Pat Riley-coached, Patrick Ewing-led Knicks took two of the next three to extend the Bulls to a Game 7.

Scottie Pippen and Michael Jordan formed perhaps the greatest two-player tandem in NBA history. Together they've won six championship rings.

This precarious, win-or-go-home position was something the Bulls did not experience during a 15–2 postseason joy ride a year earlier. Fortunately for Chicago, Pippen recorded his second career playoff triple double in Game 7 with 17 points, 11 rebounds and 11 assists, and the Bulls coasted, 110–81.

**"I thought Michael had 2,000 moves. I was wrong. He has 3,000."
–Clyde Drexler**

After disposing of the Cleveland Cavaliers in a six-game Eastern Conference Finals, the Bulls met the Portland Trail Blazers in the NBA Finals. Jordan would be matched against Clyde Drexler, the scoring guard with powers widely considered second-best in the NBA only to his.

In Game 1, Michael made sure Drexler knew who would be the boss from the opening tip. Jordan poured in 35 points and an NBA Finals record-tying six three-point baskets in the first half alone as the Bulls opened up a 66–51 lead. Jordan finished with 39 overall as the Bulls won, 122–89, and missed setting a Finals record for largest victory margin by only two points.

However, the Bulls lost their focus again in Game 2 and Portland's 115–104 victory in overtime tied the series. If the Trail Blazers won all of their next three at home, Chicago would be unseated as champion.

With not much more room for failure and the series tied at two going into Game 5, Jordan came up clutch again. He rang up 46 points and Pippen collected 24 points, 11 rebounds and nine assists for a 119–106 victory.

Back home for Game 6, the Bulls faced a 79–64 deficit entering the fourth quarter. This time, the bench ignited the Bulls on a 14–2 run early in final period. Then Jordan combined with Pippen to score their team's last 19 points in a 97–93 victory that triggered a celebration at Chicago Stadium.

After the Bulls won their first title, Jordan had said, "We wanted it for the people of Chicago."

This time, he said, "This one is for the players and the coaches."

Jordan outscored Drexler by an average of 11 points per game, amassing the second-highest scoring total for a six-game NBA Finals with 35.8 points per game to go with 6.5 assists and 4.8 rebounds.

It was 1990–91 all over again: the Bulls were champions and Jordan was the Finals' Most Valuable Player.

"Going into the series, I thought Michael had 2,000 moves," said Drexler. "I was wrong. He has 3,000."

"Jordan is the best there ever was," said Portland's Buck Williams. "No question about it. When they need him, he produces. You can't stop him. The pressure on him is unbelievable, but he still comes through."

1992 PLAYOFF RESULTS

(Home team in CAPS)

EASTERN CONFERENCE FIRST ROUND
Chicago 3, Miami 0
CHICAGO 113, Miami 94
CHICAGO 120, Miami 90
Chicago 119, MIAMI 114

EASTERN CONFERENCE SEMIFINALS
Chicago 4, New York 3
New York 94, CHICAGO 89
CHICAGO 86, New York 78
Chicago 94, NEW YORK 86
NEW YORK 93, Chicago 86
CHICAGO 96, New York 88
NEW YORK 100, Chicago 86
CHICAGO 110, New York 81

EASTERN CONFERENCE FINALS
Chicago 4, Cleveland 2
CHICAGO 103, Cleveland 89
Cleveland 107, CHICAGO 81
Chicago 105, CLEVELAND 96
CLEVELAND 99, Chicago 85
CHICAGO 112, Cleveland 89
Chicago 99, CLEVELAND 94

NBA FINALS
Chicago 4, Portland 2
CHICAGO 122, Portland 89
Portland 115, CHICAGO 104(2OT)
Chicago 94, PORTLAND 84
PORTLAND 93, Chicago 88
Chicago 119, PORTLAND 106
CHICAGO 97, Portland 93

Unstoppa-Bull!

The march of the 1995–96 Chicago Bulls to the greatest record in NBA history began with a simple two-word pronouncement that delighted the basketball world, March 18, 1995.

"I'm back," said the world's greatest player, Michael Jordan. Jordan finally had enough of swinging at (and often missing) baseballs as a member of the minor league Birmingham Barons and was ready to resume being a hero in Chicago, in the sport that he had dominated. The Bulls were delighted to have their leader back.

Jordan, reenergized and challenged by skeptics who wondered what he had lost while being away, came back in time for the final 17 regular-season games in 1994–95. Michael felt certain that he would shed his rust quickly and carry Chicago to its first title since his last season, 1992–93. But he was wrong. The Bulls' playoff run ended with elimination in the Eastern Conference Semifinals at the hands of the Orlando Magic and left Jordan stewing in his competitive juices.

Michael began a schedule of regular offseason workouts for the first time in his illustrious career. He retooled his offensive game, making a concession to age and a slight dip in his remarkable ability to soar over defenders. To minimize the pounding that accompanied his rim-attacking flights of fancy, Jordan proved he could post his usual peerless offensive numbers by leaning harder on a deadly mid-range jumper.

The league should have known that the Bulls and Jordan were not fooling around when Michael scored 42 points in a season-opening rout of Charlotte. Jordan was unstoppable, punishing Philadelphia's Jerry Stackhouse—the slashing player some people were touting as "the next Jordan"—for 48 points on Jan. 13 and notching an NBA season-high 53 against Detroit and Grant Hill on March 7.

At age 33, in his 11th pro season, Jordan averaged 30.4 points, 6.6 rebounds, 4.3 assists and 2.2 steals per game. He won his NBA-record eighth scoring title, surpassing

1995-96 CHICAGO BULLS

	G	FG%	FT%	PPG
Michael Jordan	82	.495	.834	30.4
Scottie Pippen	77	.463	.679	19.4
Toni Kukoc	81	.490	.772	13.1
Luc Longley	62	.482	.777	9.1
Steve Kerr	82	.506	.929	8.4
Ron Harper	80	.467	.705	7.4
Dennis Rodman	64	.480	.528	5.5
Bill Wennington	71	.493	.860	5.3
Jack Haley	1	.333	.500	5.0
John Salley*	17	.343	.600	2.1
Jud Buechler	74	.463	.636	3.8
Dickey Simpkins	60	.481	.629	3.6
James Edwards	28	.373	.615	3.5
Jason Caffey	57	.438	.588	3.2
Randy Brown	68	.406	.609	2.7

* Totals with Bulls only.

the mark of seven held by Wilt Chamberlain. He won the regular-season MVP Award for the fourth time.

"I may not be as physically gifted as I once was, but I think the mental aspect overrides it," said Jordan. "I am sure people are still scared of me. I do shoot a lot more jump shots, but I take what the defense gives me."

Jordan was back. However, to make history, he would need more help than his All-Star sidekick Scottie Pippen—the brilliant passer, scorer and defensively superb small forward who averaged 19.4 points and 5.9 assists per game in 1995–96—could provide by himself.

The bold addition of Dennis Rodman was another key to restoring the luster of greatness to this Chicago franchise. Before the 1995–96 season, the Bulls risked their chemistry by trading for Rodman, whose erratic behavior had extended beyond his two-title stay with the Detroit Pistons of the late 1980s.

The Bulls desperately needed a power forward to plug the hole created by Horace Grant's departure via free agency, so Chicago's Vice President of Basketball Operations Jerry Krause took a chance on Rodman. Hoping the rebounding and defensive specialist with the flamboyant lifestyle would be a contributor and not a distraction, the Bulls sent Will Perdue to San Antonio for Rodman.

Rodman was on his best behavior for most of the season and won his fifth straight NBA rebounding title, with 14.9 per game. The move wound up earning Krause NBA Executive of the Year honors.

The addition of Dennis Rodman, who holds the NBA record for most consecutive seasons (seven) leading the league in rebounds per game, gave the Bulls the interior toughness and board strength they lacked.

Rounding out the starting five were Australian center Luc Longley, for size in the middle, and the resurgent Ron Harper, who transformed himself from a defunct scoring force into a valuable defender.

The Bulls' bench featured dedicated role players. Chief among them were outside threats Toni Kukoc (87 three-pointers on .403 accuracy), the three-time European Player of the Year and NBA Sixth Man of the Year in 1995–96, and three-point magician Kerr (122 threes for a .515 mark).

How dominant were these Bulls? So dominant that their biggest challenge for months was remaining interested.

Between Nov. 27 and Dec. 23, the Bulls ran off 13 wins in a row, by an average margin of 11.2 points. After Chicago lost to Indiana and dropped to 23–3 on Dec. 26, the Bulls ran

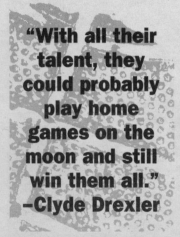

"With all their talent, they could probably play home games on the moon and still win them all." –Clyde Drexler

off an incredible club-record 18 more triumphs in a row, by an average margin of 16.4 points, for a 41–3 record. January became the first undefeated month in franchise history (14–0). The Bulls outscored opponents 105.2–92.9 for the season.

These Bulls lost two games in a row only once during the regular season. They set a club record for most consecutive road wins, with nine. They lost only twice in 41 regular-season games at the United Center and set an NBA record for most consecutive home wins, with 44 over two seasons.

"With all their talent, they could probably play home games on the moon and still win them all," said Houston Rockets star Clyde Drexler.

It all added up to a 72–10 finish that was unprecedented in NBA annals. The Bulls shattered the all-time record of the 1971–72 Los Angeles Lakers with their 70th victory,

86–80, at Milwaukee on April 16, with two games to spare in their quest for the history books.

"We're the best ever, at least the best of my era," said Pippen. "I was seven years old when the Lakers won 69 games. If they want to meet us on the court tomorrow, let's get it on."

"It's important to remember that 70 games won and no championship does not mean much at the end of the day," said Jordan. "If we don't win it all, we will be remembered as the team that won 70 games and then choked in the play-offs."

There was no choke. The Bulls swept the Miami Heat in the opening round, then took four of five from the New York Knicks. Finally, the Bulls avenged their series loss to

The Bulls capped their amazing journey—72-10 in the regular season, 15-3 during the playoffs—with yet another championship. Michael, as always, led the way.

Orlando the previous year by sweeping Shaquille O'Neal, Penny Hardaway and the Magic in the Eastern Conference Finals. Fighting an upset stomach and a sore right ankle, Jordan scored 45 points in the clincher.

Next came the Seattle SuperSonics, with Gary Payton and Shawn Kemp, in the NBA Finals. The Bulls won the first three games, pushing their playoff run to 14–1. However, the Sonics won the next two, forcing the series back to Chicago.

In Game 6, with Jordan notching 22 points, nine rebounds and seven assists, the Bulls emerged with their 87th victory in 100 games overall. As the final seconds ticked off the Bulls' 87–75 triumph in front of a delirious United Center crowd, an exhausted Jordan took the ball from Toni Kukoc.

Jordan was the only one to play in all of the Bulls' 100 games, other than Kerr, and Kerr did not approach Jordan's 3,823 total minutes played. In the postseason, Jordan had led Chicago in scoring 17 times in 18 games and had averaged 30.7 points, 4.0 rebounds, 4.1 assists and 2.2 steals.

As the buzzer sounded, Michael rolled around on the floor and cried. The Bulls' fourth title in six years, clinched on Father's Day, was dedicated to the memory of his father James, who had been murdered in 1993.

Jordan, having added Finals MVP to his regular-season MVP and All-Star Game MVP honors, had made it all the way back, better than ever.

UNSTOPPA-BULL!

1996 PLAYOFF RESULTS
(Home team in CAPS)

EASTERN CONFERENCE FIRST ROUND
Chicago 3, Miami 0
CHICAGO 102, Miami 85
CHICAGO 106, Miami 75
Chicago 112, MIAMI 91

EASTERN CONFERENCE SEMIFINALS
Chicago 4, New York 1
CHICAGO 91, New York 84
CHICAGO 91, New York 80
NEW YORK 102, Chicago 99(2OT)
Chicago 94, NEW YORK 91
CHICAGO 94, New York 81

EASTERN CONFERENCE FINALS
Chicago 4, Orlando 0
CHICAGO 121, Orlando 83
CHICAGO 93, Orlando 88
Chicago 86, ORLANDO 67
Chicago 106, ORLANDO 101

NBA FINALS
Chicago 4, Seattle 2
CHICAGO 107, Seattle 90
CHICAGO 92, Seattle 88
Chicago 108, SEATTLE 86
SEATTLE 107, Chicago 86
SEATTLE 89, Chicago 78
CHICAGO 87, Seattle 75